Original title:
Tropical Light

Copyright © 2025 Creative Arts Management OÜ
All rights reserved.

Author: Rosalie Bradford
ISBN HARDBACK: 978-1-80581-519-8
ISBN PAPERBACK: 978-1-80581-046-9
ISBN EBOOK: 978-1-80581-519-8

Warm Embrace of Day

Sunshine spills like melted cheese,
Lizards dance with feline ease.
Parrots squawk their morning cheer,
While coconuts drop, oh dear!

Light Through the Canopy

Dappled paths play tag with shade,
Monkeys swing, a wild parade.
Under leaves, a secret show,
Where all the funny critters go!

Coral Caress

Fish donning colors, bright and loud,
Swim past coral, feeling proud.
Jellyfish waltz, a gooey glide,
While sea turtles wear their pride!

A Glimpse of Paradise

Flip-flops squeak on sandy shores,
Where laughter echoes, never bores.
A beach ball bounces, fun in sight,
As seagulls mug for scraps, so polite!

Jungle's Heartbeat

In the jungle where the monkeys play,
The parrots squawk in a joyful fray.
A snake slithers by with a comical grin,
As the frogs hop in, let the antics begin.

Underneath the swaying palm leaves' sway,
A lizard dances, boasting all day.
The toucans flap with a silly style,
While the sloths move slow, adding to the smile.

Morning chorus of Colors

The sun ticks up, a golden delight,
Butterflies bloom, what a colorful sight.
Cacophony of sounds, all in good cheer,
Even the flowers giggle, 'We're glad you're here!'

A chameleon struts with flair galore,
Changing shades just to settle the score.
As the day breaks, there's laughter abound,
In this vibrant land, joy can be found.

Blissful Mirage

A shimmering haze makes the lizards prance,
As they think they're part of a dazzling dance.
With a flip and a wiggle, they join the parade,
    While the iguanas chuckle, unafraid.

The heat brings out mischief, playful jest,
  As the critters partake in their lively fest.
They sip on sweet nectar, with laughter, they gleam,
  In a world of mirages, life's more than a dream.

Nectar of the Sun

Buzzing bees wear the funniest hats,
While sipping sweet nectar, oh how they chat!
The flowers gossip about their bright hues,
As the sun laughs along, sharing the news.

A turtle flips over, laughing in glee,
He shouts, 'Who's faster? You or me?'
With every drop of sunshine that glows,
Even the drab shades come out for some shows.

Uplifted Spirits

The sun's a giant disco ball,
Spinning rays that make us fall.
Birds wear shades and sing out loud,
Even flowers dance in a crowd.

Coconuts drop like confetti,
While squirrels in shorts look so petty.
A breeze tickles every nose,
As laughter blooms like summer's rose.

Kaleidoscopic Day

Colors clash like a paint fight,
Parrots chat with pure delight.
Flip-flops slap on sandy shores,
As crabs crawl like they own the floors.

Rainbows burst, oh what a scene!
Lizards strut like they're on a screen.
A sunburnt dad wears a smile,
Sun hats spinning in for a while.

Vibrations of Summer

The melons laugh, they're ripe and round,
While ants throw parties underground.
Ice cream drips on wacky hats,
And seagulls joke about the bats.

The beach ball bounces high and wide,
As kids leap in with joyful pride.
Sunblock slips, a slippery game,
Splashing water, wild and tame.

Nature's Glow

Fireflies flirt with evening's sigh,
As frogs perform their great alarm cry.
A picnic basket bursts with cheer,
Guess who forgot the drinks this year?

The stars wear shades, they twinkle bright,
Bugs dance close, in pure delight.
Underneath the moonlit tree,
Laughter floats, oh so carefree.

Daybreak's Embrace

A rooster sings, it's time to rise,
The sun peeks out, oh what a prize!
Pajamas fly in morning breeze,
While coffee spills with flurry and tease!

Napping cats chase shadows long,
The dance begins, we sing a song!
Flip-flops clapping on the floor,
Who knew morning could be such a chore?

Golden Reflections

Mirrors of the sea, so slick and bright,
Fish in tuxedos swim left and right.
Parrots squawk their jokes so loud,
As sunburned tourists gather round.

Sandy toes and ice cream drips,
Seashells worn like fancy blips.
With every wave, a splashy fate,
Oh, what a ride - don't be too late!

Dappled Radiance

On the hammock, I softly swing,
Chasing naps is my favorite thing.
Coconut caught in tangled hair,
How did that happen? I swear it's rare!

Lemonade spills on the sunburned grass,
Bees buzz by, they're quite the class!
Caught in a giggle, a slip and a trip,
It's just another fun-filled summer trip!

Aquatic Glimmers

The poolside chairs, a splash parade,
Dive right in, it's time to cascade!
Rubber ducks race down the way,
Oh look at that one, it's gone astray!

The sunblock wars are in full swing,
Who knew lotion could have such bling?
Squeaky floats and beach ball strife,
Such is the joy of summer life!

Sunkissed Serenity

On a beach where flip-flops sing,
Seagulls dance, and children swing.
A sunburned nose, a laughing tide,
In sunscreen we trust, we take a ride.

Ice cream cones, they melt away,
Sticky hands at the end of the day.
Funny hats upon our heads,
While crabs tiptoe on the sandy beds.

Horizon of Dreams

Kites are flying, bright and free,
Over the waves, as far as we see.
A parrot squawks a silly tune,
While kids chase jellyfish in the afternoon.

Riding waves with pancake flips,
Sailing boats, and playful quips.
There's laughter echoing all around,
As coconut falls and rolls on the ground.

Opalescent Skies

Clouds like cotton candy swirl,
As surfers practice their perfect twirl.
Each sunset bursts with the loudest cheer,
While everyone sneezes—the pollen is here!

Bikinis bright, like rainbows bold,
Sandy pails of treasures untold.
Old men nap with tweezers in hand,
Dreaming of fish caught in the sand.

Twilight Harmony

Evening falls with a wink and a grin,
As fireflies join the party to spin.
Hot dogs roasting, laughter loud,
While grandma's napkin turns her proud.

Laughter lingers, fun will flow,
Mismatched socks in the afterglow.
Under the stars, we all collide,
With bug spray on, we take the ride.

Radiant Petals

In a garden where the sun does wink,
Bright colors bloom, and flowers think.
Petals giggle in the sunny tease,
Dancing lightly on the warm breeze.

Bees in shades of striped delight,
Join the party from morn till night.
They buzz along, a silly crew,
Painting the sky in yellow and blue.

Cascade of Color

A paintbrush spills on the grassy floor,
Splashes of red, and a little more.
The trees wear hats in shades so bold,
And laugh as their trunks stay bright and old.

Lemon clouds float without a care,
Tickling the air, oh what a flair!
Fruits hang low with a zesty grin,
Shouting, "Come join, let the fun begin!"

Hues of Harmony

A rainbow slid down from the sky,
Landed on fish with a splashy sigh.
They wiggle in water, all colors bright,
Making a scene of a joyful sight.

Parrots gossip with squawky flair,
Swinging on branches like they just don't care.
With each flap, they'd shuffle and hop,
Creating laughter that never would stop.

Whispered Reflections

In a puddle, the sun drops by,
Winks at frogs as they croak and sigh.
Reflections giggle, a playful ring,
Splashing back tales that the ripples sing.

Monkeys swing low with a cheeky grin,
Throwing fruit at each other's chin.
Laughter echoes through leafy halls,
Where every stone holds a secret that calls.

The Realm of Sunrays

In a land where shadows dare not play,
Sunbeams prance in a golden ballet.
Lizards wear hats, oh what a sight,
Dancing in splendor, feeling just right.

Frogs on lily pads sing silly songs,
While butterflies flit and join the throngs.
Every flower wears a smile so wide,
In this laugh-filled world, there's no need to hide.

Sanctuary of Colors

Jellybean trees grow up to the sky,
Where gumdrop birds frequently fly.
Painted skies giggle, hues in a swirl,
As rainbow fish in the pool do twirl.

Cotton candy clouds drift by with glee,
Tickling the sun for a cup of tea.
A kaleidoscope of fun, such a sight,
In this sanctuary, everything's light.

Bursting Blossoms

Tulips wear ties, daisies dance bold,
Each petal a story, a secret untold.
Squirrels in bowties do hop and spin,
While the bees pollinate under a grin.

Blooming laughter, fragrant with cheer,
Ticklish breezes whisper in your ear.
Nature's joke is a raucous rhyme,
Bursting with colors, transcending time.

Illumination in the Breeze

A cornucopia spins in the air,
With giggles and chuckles, no single care.
Lights flicker, winking like stars at noon,
Fluffy clouds bounce to a bouncy tune.

Dancing leaves perform pirouettes fine,
While shadows laugh in an endless line.
Every gust carries a chuckling tease,
In this world of whimsy, made to please.

Dancing Shadows

In the garden, shadows sway,
Bouncing like they wish to play,
Lizards slip and hop around,
Making giggles with each bound.

A crab with lunatic grace,
Dances sideways, what a face!
Sunbeams tickle every leaf,
Nature's laughter, pure relief.

Palm fronds wave, the breeze sings,
While the parrots chat on swings,
A squirrel's tail like a flag,
In this fun, we fit like a rag!

With a wink, the day slips by,
As the sun pulls up the sky,
Merriment in every sight,
Dance with shadows into night.

Blissful Horizon

Mermaids giggle, lost at sea,
Jellyfish, just giggling, whee!
Waves crash, clumsily they clap,
Salt spray's like a birthday cap.

Sunsets wear a silly grin,
Colors twist and then they spin,
Turtles laugh in slow-motion,
Splashing joy with clumsy devotion.

A coconut falls, oh what a sound,
Nutty laughter all around,
Seagulls swoop with comic flair,
Chasing dreams through salty air.

Stars appear, a wink and a cheer,
Guiding everyone to here,
Horizon smiles, a cheeky sight,
Even the moon joins in delight.

Island Gleam

Amidst the palm trees, mischief thrums,
A party where the coconut hums,
Starfish wear hats, they strut and sway,
Inviting us to join the play.

With hula hoops made from the sea,
Dancing dolphins shout, 'Come see!'
Flip-flops flying through the air,
As island breezes play with hair.

On sandy shores, the crabs run wild,
Each with a grin like a playful child,
They're breakdance kings with claws out wide,
In this gleam, we take our ride!

Golden rays glimmer with glee,
As we laugh 'til we have to flee,
In the whispers of the breeze,
Joy rides high, it's such a tease!

Aetherial Dawn

Morning sun starts with a wink,
Birds chirp, making us think,
Cups of coffee start to dance,
With sleep still in a lazy trance!

Sunglasses perched on our nose,
Fog rolls back like a slumber dose,
Lizards slip on little shoes,
Ready for the day's fresh news.

Banana peels are on the chase,
As breakfast parties fill the place,
A wild fruit salad's in the mix,
Laughter flings across like tricks.

With our hats and shades in tow,
We chase the sun and feel the glow,
In the aura of morning bright,
We laugh and dance with pure delight!

Sunlit Reverie

In the morn, the sun does peek,
Casting shadows, smiles, and squeaks.
Little critters jump and play,
While I sip my drink, hooray!

Coconut drops from above,
Landed where I'd wish to shove.
The birds are dancing in the trees,
While I swat at buzzing bees.

Lemon-squirted laughter flies,
As I chase a rolling pie.
Palm leaves whisper silly tunes,
To the rhythm of bright loons.

Bouncing sunbeams on the sand,
Merry chaos, oh so grand.
Life's a circus, bright and loud,
Here I stand, a jester proud.

Nature's Brightest Tapestry

Woven greens and splashes bright,
Lemon yellows, pure delight.
Silly flowers tease the sun,
Making every moment fun.

Bumbling bees in playful flight,
Buzz around with sheer delight.
While dancing leaves in breezy air,
Whisper secrets none would share.

A chattering lizard does a twirl,
While nearby, a bright shell swirls.
Crabs in suits of shells and glide,
Oh, such silly seaside pride!

With every chirp and poke and pluck,
Nature laughs, oh what luck!
Amidst this crafted chaos free,
I find joy and pure glee.

Floral Symphony

Petals yelp in hues so loud,
Tickling bees, they dance, so proud.
Swaying hips of flora greet,
With fragrance mild and spice so sweet.

Bouncing blooms in sunny grace,
With ladybugs in a race.
A hop, a skip, and then a fall,
Nature laughs, oh, we all call!

Jellybeans of colors bright,
Mingle in the warm sunlight.
In this garden, oh what fun,
Watch them sparkle, all day long!

Drink the nectar, drop the frown,
In this arena, joy's the crown.
With every bud and buzzing ring,
Let us laugh and let us sing!

Oasis of Dreams

In the shade of a palm, so green,
I found a snack most unforeseen.
A monkey with a straw hat on,
Sipping juice till the break of dawn.

Laughter carried on a breeze,
Swaying as if with perfect ease.
A parrot squawking out a tune,
Made me giggle, oh so soon!

Flip-flops flapping on the sand,
As I buried my friend's feet, quite planned.
He laughed and shouted, "I'm a crab!"
As we both fell into the fab.

Underneath the starry sheen,
We danced a jig, feeling like a teen.
In this paradise, we find our glee,
Who knew such fun could be so free?

Celestial Paradiso

The sun made my ice cream melt,
As sticky fingers joyfully felt.
I chased a seagull for a bite,
But tripped over a sandcastle, quite the sight!

Shells and treasures all around,
I wore a crown of seaweed, quite renowned.
The tide snuck up, my shoes took flight,
And squeals erupted with sheer delight.

A crab declared it all a feast,
While sunbathers just laughed at the beast.
He scuttled off with a grand old cheer,
Leaving us rolling in sand, oh dear!

Underneath the cotton clouds,
We celebrated with giggles and shrouds.
This place felt like the best surprise,
Where silliness wears the brightest guise.

Enchanted Lightscape

A lighthouse standing with a grin,
A gnome had a party, let's begin!
With leafy hats and fruit for all,
We spun around, feeling ten feet tall.

Sipping drinks from coconut cups,
Every sip had us giggling up.
A flamingo joined our silly game,
Twirling about, what a wild name!

The sunset painted the sky a peach,
As I tried to learn a tango, but screeched.
A crab yelled, "You've got two left feet!"
And the crowd roared, "Still dance to the beat!"

With every bounce, we danced anew,
The stars above seemed to laugh too.
This lightscape filled with jest and cheer,
Made each moment feel so dear!

Sunlit Retreat

In a hammock swung with grace,
I dozed off, but dreamed of race.
Chasing after limes on the floor,
Stumbled right into a beach galore.

With laughter bubbling like the brew,
I built a tower, silly but true.
Then a wave knocked it into the sea,
And I yelled, "That's my property!"

Flip-flops flying, toes in the sand,
My dog joined in, so full of grand.
He dug up treasures, bones, oh my!
A parrot squawked, "You can't deny!"

Under the sun, we played all day,
With laughter echoing, come what may.
In this retreat, joy found its beat,
Life feels best with fun and heat!

Elysian Dawn

When the sun yawns wide, it's time to play,
Bikini tops and sun hats on display.
The roosters crow like they're in a race,
While coconuts fall, at a dizzying pace.

Flip-flops dancing on the sandy track,
Seagulls squawking, 'Hey, don't go back!'
Mangoes wink as they roll down the lane,
And lizards gossip about last night's rain.

A fruity smoothie steals the show,
As surfers line up like a circus row.
With splashes echoing joy in the air,
And sunscreen shenanigans everywhere.

So raise your glass to this comical morn,
In a land where worries are happily shorn.
With laughter bouncing from beach to bay,
Elysian Dawn will keep blues at bay.

Whispering Palms

Palms sway as if sharing a joke,
While tourists trip over their own poke.
A breeze whispers secrets of sunbaked sand,
And flip-flops fly from a sunburned hand.

Bikinis bright like a party of fish,
While pineapple hats fulfill wishes, oh swish!
Crabs do a tango, old man in tow,
As snorkelers search for a fishy woe.

Every shadow seems to giggle and play,
As life becomes one big light-hearted ballet.
With coconuts chuckling like old pals tight,
In the land where each moment is pure delight.

So let each leaf's laughter fill the air,
In this witty realm, devoid of despair.
Whispering palms know how joy can bloom,
Lighting up hearts like flowers in a room.

Sunlit Canopy

Under canopies lush with sassy greens,
Chasing sunbeams and carefree scenes.
Toucan call out, 'What's the big deal?'
As iguanas lounge, taking a meal.

The monkeys swing like they're on a spree,
While butterflies flutter, wild and free.
Each moment a chuckle, nature's own show,
With leaves that rustle as if in the know.

A hammock sways, and so do we,
Measuring giggles and cups of tea.
With sunsets painting the funny facade,
It's the walls that will only seem odd.

So let's clap hands for this jovial space,
Where sunshine and silliness interlace.
In the sunlit canopy, laughter is found,
A comedy club without a bound.

Luminous Shores

Waves roll in with a boisterous cheer,
As beach balls bounce, it's quite the atmosphere.
Children giggle, building castles askew,
While realizing they're just big mud goo.

The lifeguard lounged with a book on his chest,
As gulls swoop low, they think they're the best.
With surfboards leaning like tipsy friends,
And sunscreen mischief that never ends.

A seashell offers a story or two,
Of salty adventures from ocean's blue.
Mermaids laugh with their shimmering tails,
Underneath silly, flapping sails.

So kick off your shoes, let the fun take flight,
As luminous shores toast to sheer delight.
In this quirky playground, joy reigns high,
With every wave crashing, laugh 'til you cry.

Aetherial Waters

In a pool of wobbly jelly,
Ducks wear shades, oh so silly.
Fish pull pranks with a splash,
While sunbeams giggle and dash.

Rubber ducks float in a row,
Sipping lemonade, oh what a show!
Frogs croak jokes on a lily pad,
With laughter so loud it makes them glad.

The otter's slip, a comical sight,
Chasing reflections in pure delight.
A mermaid grins, don't take her bait,
Snack time is here, let's celebrate!

Bubbles burst with a giggle and pop,
In these waters, the fun never stops.
With laughter afloat and joy in the air,
Who knew such bliss was hiding down there?

Glowing Canopies

Under leaves that dance and sway,
Monkeys swing in a playful fray.
Squirrels juggle acorns with flair,
While sunbeams giggle, never a care.

The parrot tells puns from the sky,
"Why did the mango refuse to lie?"
"Because it was ripe with the truth!" he's sure,
And the trees laugh back, "We need more of that cure!"

Chasing shadows on the forest floor,
Caterpillars crawl, but who's keeping score?
Fireflies flash, like a disco ball,
They light the night, as night creatures call.

With coconuts dropping and laughter in flight,
This canopy's glow is pure delight.
The breeze whispers jokes that make us grin,
In every shadow, a silly win!

Elixir of Sunshine

Sip the nectar from the sun,
In this party, we're all just fun!
Tigers dance, oh what a sight,
While the rhymes of roosters take flight.

Coconuts wear tiny hats,
While llamas organize acrobats.
Toasting with fruit punch so bold,
The secrets of happiness unfold.

Hummingbirds zoom with a flair,
Tickling noses, we squeal and stare.
Giraffes stretch tall to catch a breeze,
Tickled pink by the chatter of bees.

Every sip brings a comic cheer,
Funny faces from those near.
In this elixir, joy we find,
With every sip, we're all entwined!

Echoes of a Warm Breeze

A warm breeze whispers jokes aloud,
Carrying laughter from the crowd.
Palm trees sway, they join the jest,
In a comedy that's simply the best.

Sandy shores with wiggly toes,
Seagulls gossip in silly prose.
"Why did the crab pinch the pie?" it sings,
"Because it wanted to wear fancy blings!"

The sun tickles the ocean's face,
Adding giggles to the sandy space.
Shells chuckle as waves crash near,
Their secrets ripple, loud and clear.

In this warm breeze, fun's never shy,
It spins around as the moments fly.
With echoes of joy drifting free,
We dance along, wild and carefree!

Cockatoo Calls at Dusk

Cockatoos squawk, a playful band,
Dancing with shadows, oh so grand.
They've stolen the sunset, what a sight,
Making a ruckus, all through the night.

They flap and hop with quirky flair,
In their party hats, such a wild affair.
Juicy fruit treats in their beaks,
Making funny faces, the laughs peak!

Up in the trees, they chatter away,
Plotting mischief for the next day.
With a wink and a wink, they take their flight,
As dusk wraps the world in soft delight.

Embracing the Day

Sunrise tickles with a gleeful ray,
Chasing sleeping clouds away.
Birds in pajamas, chirping loud,
Each laugh a note in the morning crowd.

Butterflies waltz on the breeze so light,
Spreading joy in a grand delight.
They sip the nectar, oh what a treat,
Dance in the sun with silly feet!

Laughter bubbles in the air,
Nature's giggles without a care.
Embracing the day in vibrant hues,
With a wink to the world, saying "I choose!"

Zephyr's Delight

A breeze dances in a swirling dress,
Tickling the trees, they laugh and confess.
The flowers nod with a playful grin,
As zephyrs whisper, inviting you in.

Kites soar high, like dreams set free,
With squeals of joy wrapped in glee.
Frogs leap and croak in clownish shows,
Joining the chorus of nature's prose.

Children at play, their giggles abound,
Turning the park into joyous ground.
With every gust, antics unfold,
In the gentle breeze, stories are told.

Vivid Sunshine

Golden beams splash across the scene,
Painting the world, so bright and serene.
Squirrels skitter, chasing at speed,
As silly antics become their creed.

The beach balls bounce, a whimsical sight,
Flip-flops flying in delight!
Sandcastles wobble, with laughter perched,
As kids build dreams, their joy is searched.

Ice cream drips with comical flair,
A rainbow of flavors, scents fill the air.
Vivid colors make the day unfold,
In sunshine's warmth, the fun never gets old.

Brilliance on the Breeze

Colors whirly like a dance,
Sunshine's giggles in a trance.
Palm trees sway with silly glee,
As coconuts drop down for tea.

Lizards lounge upon the chair,
Wearing shades, without a care.
Crabs in bow ties strut their stuff,
Chasing seagulls, oh so tough!

Bright umbrellas, colors clash,
Picnics turn to messy splash.
Waves that tickle every toe,
Sandcastles with a funky glow.

Joy is wrapped in sun-soaked wraps,
Silly hats and well-worn maps.
Underneath that golden ball,
Life's a jest, let's laugh through all!

Serene Sunrise

Morning's wink, a chuckle bright,
Laughter spills in warm daylight.
Birds in hats sing silly tunes,
While fish wear ties and dance like loons.

The coffee brews with cheeky flair,
A steamy wave sits in mid-air.
Toasters toast with jokes to share,
Pop-tarts wander, unaware.

Sunflowers grin, they know the score,
Tickling bees in a buzzing roar.
The hammock sways, a nap's decree,
Dreams of puddles, oh, just for me!

With bright balloons that float up high,
Each puff of wind, a gleeful sigh.
Morning dances with kooky style,
In a light that makes us smile!

Embered Clouds

Cotton candy skies above,
Marshmallow dreams, a lighthearted love.
Silly squirrels in hats of fur,
Jump and giggle, what's the stir?

Fireflies twinkle, throwing shade,
Playing pranks, they're not afraid.
One lights up, the other's shy,
Zipping past, they wave bye-bye!

Sunset's glow, a comic show,
Chuckling colors, what a flow!
Bananas slip upon the ground,
As giggles echo all around.

Eyes wide open in pure delight,
Chasing dreams, oh what a sight!
Even the stars join in the fun,
Under this world, we laugh and run!

Vibrant Silhouettes

Sunset draws with crayons bright,
Painting shadows in the night.
Dancers sprinkle laughter's dust,
As fireflies gather, it's a must!

Silly shapes upon the shore,
Frogs in tuxes, what a score!
Lemonade rainbows, cheers abound,
Beachballs bounce with joyful sound.

Palms are swaying, hands in air,
Keeping rhythm, without a care.
Surfboards laughing on their rides,
As giggling waves create wild slides.

Nighttime whispers funny tales,
Of pizza parties and silly snails.
Every star a wink and grin,
In this dance, let laughter win!

Warmth Beneath the Palms

Sandy toes and a playful breeze,
Fruits that dance on the swaying trees.
Coconuts sing, they spill their jokes,
While sunburned tourists, well, they poke!

Laughter lingers like a sweet sunburn,
Beach towels tangled, oh, when will we learn?
Seagulls dive for leftover fries,
While we sip drinks with tiny umbrellas on the rise.

Flip-flops flying, what a hilarious sight,
Someone gets stuck, now that's pure delight!
With shades on noses, we strike a pose,
And hope the tide won't take our clothes!

The heat brings smiles and silly grins,
While jokes and sunburns compete to win.
Under palm leaves, we all shall meet,
For fun deserves a sunny seat.

Enchanted Sunset

Painted skies in a riot of hues,
The golden hour teases like mischievous blues.
The sun tips its hat, what a show,
While self-timed selfies steal the glow!

Sipping cocktails like a summer swan,
My hat flew off, oh where has it gone?
Laughter echoes with the waves' embrace,
Nature chuckles, it knows our place.

Crickets chirp their funny little tune,
As I stumble on shells beneath the moon.
Barefoot and giggly, we dance in line,
As dusk drapes us in a glow divine.

With the day's end, we cheer and sigh,
Each sunset laugh a reason to fly.
Memories made with a toast so grand,
To the chaos of life on a sun-kissed land.

Radiant Reverie

Under the rays where the wild things play,
A parrot squawks jokes in his colorful way.
I chuckle at crabs doing their dance,
While tourists fumble in sweet romance.

Sun-kissed cocktails, oh what a mix,
The blender's laughter, the perfect fix!
With quirky hats and mismatched styles,
We prance like goofballs, winning all the smiles.

An iguana peers with a curious eye,
While I try to limbo and nearly fly!
Palm leaves make shadows where giggles grow,
Sunshine and humor, the ultimate show.

With every splash and every jest,
Life's funny side puts us to the test.
In this bright world, we laugh with glee,
In a heated chaos, forever carefree.

Nature's Illuminated Canvas

Brushstrokes of green on a canvas so wide,
With critters that waddle, we giggle and glide.
Bumblebees buzzing like they know the score,
While flowers play tricks with a pollen encore.

Beaches baldly flaunt their finest sand,
A crab parade, oh isn't it grand?
With each little wave, a tickle or two,
Silly sea creatures dance just for you.

Waves whisper secrets with foamy delight,
As flip-flops betray us, what a sight!
The sun sets the stage for nightly pranks,
While we recount joys as the nighttime drank.

Fireflies laugh in a glittering swarm,
And we join the dance, oh how we perform!
Nature's palette, in jest, we meet,
For life is a canvas when you're light on your feet.

Color Burst in Paradise

In a land where the fruits wear a smile,
Coconuts giggle, they dance for a while.
While mangoes jump, they slip on a peel,
Pineapples chuckle, oh what a deal!

Seashells are laughing, they tickle the sand,
And waves play tricks, oh ain't it so grand?
Gazing at sunset, a clown fish sways,
In this colorful world, we spend our days.

Dancing with shadows, we spin and we sway,
Bananas in pajamas come out to play.
Lemons tell jokes in the soft golden hue,
While lovers share giggles, a love that's so true.

Rainbows take flight on the breeze, what a sight!
A splash of confetti, oh what pure delight.
In this burst of color, joy's never afar,
Life's a zany circus, we're all the stars!

Shimmering Haven

Beneath the palm trees, the sun throws a fit,
With jellyfish doing the wobbly split.
Laughter erupts from a crab on the shore,
As seagulls squawk 'Hey! Just one joke more!'

In this shimmering space, drinks wearing umbrellas,
Frogs leap in goggles, oh what silly fellas!
Puddles of laughter reflect in the blue,
While a parrot sings songs of the wacky and new.

Bikinis and board shorts are fashion's own fun,
With ice cream that melts, but we don't seem to run.
Footprints in sand spell a tale quite absurd,
As dolphins debate on the latest birdword.

In this haven of whimsy, hearts dance in the rays,
While sunlight plays peekaboo, oh how it sways!
With giggles and splashes, we savor the bliss,
Oh shimmering haven, we couldn't resist!

Solstice Serenade

When the sun's in a hurry, just look at him go,
He's juggling the clouds for a bright little show.
As shadows get silly, they trip on the grass,
The daisies start giggling, oh how they contrast!

Under cerulean skies, our hammock's awry,
Swinging like dolphins, we frolic and fly.
Each sip of the fizz tickles just like a joke,
The pine trees are singing, we'd smile till we choked.

Flip-flops are racing, they scatter with glee,
Making merry sounds as they dance by the sea.
In this solstice of warmth, the world's quite absurd,
With whispers of laughter, it's never deterred!

So let's toast to the sun, with a wink and a cheer,
For every bright moment that keeps us all near.
In this serenade, life's never too bland,
With humor and joy, let's all take a stand!

Luminous Oasis

In the heart of the wild, where the cacti all jest,
A lizard wears glasses, he thinks he's the best.
Cactus flowers giggle, they dance in the shade,
While shadows are startled, by mischief they've made.

A parrot in polka dots sings with a flair,
As sunbeams get tangled in winds of fresh air.
With coconuts juggling, the fun doesn't stop,
While ants wear top hats, they dance and they hop.

Rippling streams are laughing, with ticklish little ways,
As frogs hold a party, in a synchronized phase.
Each ripple a giggle, each splash a bright cheer,
In this luminous spot, we forget every fear!

So raise a tall drink, let's savor the sight,
Of sneakers and sunflowers, levels of delight.
In this oasis of laughter, we'll dance 'til the night,
Oh, what a grand gathering, a pure hearted flight!

Serenity in Bloom

In a garden where bananas sway,
A parrot mimics what we say.
Lizards dance on sun-warmed stone,
While bees debate on their own throne.

A pineapple wore a silly hat,
As squirrels played hide-and-seek with the cat.
Palm trees giggle in the warm breeze,
Tickling cheeks like mischievous tease.

Coconuts chuckle, oh so round,
As iguanas lay on the ground.
The flowers wink, a sight so keen,
In this garden of glee, not mean!

So join the fun under the sun,
Where laughter blooms, and we all run.
On Saturdays, we have a feast,
With fruit salad that never ceased!

Breath of the Sunlit Sea

Waves like laughter greet the shore,
Where rubber ducks are never a bore.
Seagulls dive, like they're on a spree,
Spectators shout, "Look at me!"

Starfish pose with starry flair,
While crabs have nail polish to share.
Surfboards gossip in the sun,
As jellyfish join in the fun.

A beach ball bounces, scoring teams,
While coconuts roll with goofy dreams.
Fins and tails splash with delight,
Under the settings of golden light.

Laughter carries on salty air,
With flip-flops lost, we do not care.
The sun dips low, but oh, what a sight,
As night dances in, sparkling bright!

Golden Canopy

In jungles thick where shadows play,
Monkeys throw fruit in quirky array.
A toucan poses for a photo shoot,
While frogs pull off a funky cute.

Leaves rustle like a laughter burst,
In this forest, joy's rehearsed.
Sloths hang out, quite in their zone,
Riding vines like they own the throne.

A butterfly winks, oh so sly,
Amongst the blooms, it flutters by.
Parrots gossip about the day,
In a gossip column, come what may.

As shadows stretch, the crickets sing,
While fireflies sparkle, a magical thing.
Under the stars, in this leafy lair,
Laughter echoes, floating in the air!

Sunlit Whisper

Sunrise twirls in shades of glee,
As roosters crow a symphony.
The fruit stand sings a vibrant tune,
While limes skate by the afternoon.

Sunglasses dance on noses proud,
As sunscreen slaps, the crowd gets loud.
Flip-flops squeak and children shout,
While ice cream drips without a doubt.

The hammock sways with no retreat,
As coconut dreams sway in the heat.
A sailor's sneeze rocks the boat,
As dolphins play, a joyful note.

So here's to days that spark the heart,
With laughter that will never part.
A sun-kissed world, both bright and true,
Where every moment feels brand new!

Shimmering Trails

The sun spills gold upon the sea,
As crabs dance like they're in a spree.
Parrots squawk with jokes to share,
While monkeys clash without a care.

With flip-flops flapping, they run amok,
Building sandcastles that barely rock.
A sea turtle grins, it's quite the sight,
Waving at tourists who squint at the light.

A beach ball bounces, a wild flight,
Dodging sunburned folks left and right.
With laughter echoing through the air,
This shining day is beyond compare.

So grab a drink, with a silly straw,
And join the shenanigans, just because!
Under the glow of the giant sun,
Every moment here is pure, silly fun.

Pulses of Dawn

The rooster crows, it's time to wake,
A sleepy dog decides to shake.
With sizzling eggs and a flippant laugh,
A parrot steals a slice of staff.

The ocean waves clap, they ripple and roll,
While surfers get tangled, oh what a goal!
Splashing bright hues of creamy foam,
Chasing each other like they're back home.

Bananas drop from trees like rain,
While juggling monkeys bring the pain.
The morning sun, a golden ball,
Turns everyone into a giggling thrall.

Each quick step is met with a slip,
Watch out, my friend, don't take a trip!
In the glow of day, let laughter thrive,
This jam-packed morning keeps joy alive!

Celestial Bloom

In gardens bright where colors clash,
Frogs wear hats, some in a splash.
Bees dance around, on the hunt for fun,
While flowers giggle under the sun.

A snail races with a cunning frown,
As the sun begins to slowly drown.
Clouds puff up like marshmallow treats,
While ants march on, with tiny feats.

The dew drops wear sparkles like crowns,
As giraffes munch greens in their gowns.
The sky erupts with flaming hues,
A symphony played on buzzing blues.

In the garden's heart, laughter blooms,
Morphing troubles into cartoonish zooms.
With each sunset, the giggles bloom,
In this paradise that chases the gloom.

Incandescent Oasis

In the middle of nowhere, a pool so bright,
Makes everyone feel like a big delight.
Swim trunks flying, laughter bursts,
While flamingos dance— oh how they thirst!

Palm trees wave with a playful cheer,
While lizards strut, no sign of fear.
Splashing in water, they try to glide,
Then trip on rubber ducks that collide.

A hammock sways, caught in the tale,
With sunburned cheeks, it's a laughing gale.
As drinks with umbrellas swirl in the breeze,
Party hats wobble with the greatest ease.

So come for the fun, stay for the glow,
In this vibrant sphere of relaxation show.
Each quirky moment simply bewilders,
In this oasis where joy just filters.

Colorful Solstice

The sun wore shades, oh what a sight,
Palm trees danced, feeling just right.
Coconuts roll, chasing on sand,
Flip-flops flip, as footprints expand.

Mangoes giggle, they drop with a thud,
Sipping sweet juice, we're lost in a flood.
The beach ball bounces, a laugh and a squeal,
A crab's doing pirouettes, what a big deal!

Seagulls compete for the last fish fry,
"Mine!" they squawk, oh, what a sly guy.
Sunscreen fights, with splatters galore,
Who knew beaches could be such a chore?

Night falls softly, as stars start to peek,
Fireflies join in, with a whimsical tweak.
As we snicker at seaweed, tangled in hair,
A day full of laughter to cherish and share!

Vibrant Horizons

Kites take flight, colorful and bright,
Wiggly worms dance, such a comical sight.
Sandy toes tickle, as laughter ensues,
Crabs have a laugh in those silly blue shoes.

A parrot squawks jokes, on a coconut throne,
Funky fruit hats, who knew they'd be grown?
Giggling kids build a castle of glee,
A moat filled with turtles? Oh, let it be!

In a hammock we swing, as the breeze does sway,
Flip-flop fashion, it's the style of the day.
Laughter erupts with each goofy slip,
It's all part of the fun, on this sunny trip!

As sunset paints skies in pink and gold,
The day winds down, but never grows old.
With memories and smiles, we wave goodbye,
In this blissful realm, we'll always fly!

Verdant Glories

From ferns to flowers, a riot of hues,
A monkey swings by, dressed in the best shoes.
Laughter erupts from the sweet little stream,
Where frogs wear crowns and live in a dream.

Palm trees are wigglers, they throw a grand party,
As breezes invite us, oh isn't it hearty?
In this lively garden, all things seem spry,
Even the tarantulas pop out to say hi.

Each flower's a dancer, with petals on point,
While ants take a break at the picnic joint.
As mangoes and laughter collide in one bowl,
We toast to the mischief that fuels our soul!

When lightning bugs come out in a glow,
We join in a jig, with moves rather slow.
As night takes charge and the stars start to peek,
It's a wild and funny world, where giggles won't leak!

Celestial Caress

The moon wears a smile, gleaming and round,
While stars play tag over the warm ground.
Clouds make soft pillows, for dreams on the fly,
A jellyfish floats past, oh, my oh my!

Night markets are bustling, laughter and fries,
Fish with big wigs debating the skies.
The fortune teller winks with a hilarious twist,
"Beware of wet socks!" she adds to the list.

Glow sticks are wands in this magical night,
As we twirl and whirl, just feeling delight.
With giggles and sighs, and starlight galore,
We dance on the beach, oh, who could ask for more?

As the tide whispers secrets, calming and slow,
We chase silly shadows, just letting it flow.
In this whimsical world, where laughter won't cease,
Under starlit caresses, we find all our peace!

Verdant Vistas

Lush green hills wear sunshine hats,
Frogs sing loudly, dance like rats.
Parrots gossip with a cheeky grin,
While monkeys swing, it's time to begin.

Coconuts juggle, what a sight!
Hippos waltz in pure delight.
A seedling dreams of skyscraper heights,
While ants plot parties every night!

Silken Daybreak

Morning dew creates a slippery show,
Geckos slip, then put on a glow.
Kites are flying, and so does my shoe,
As I trip and tumble—oh, what a view!

Breezes whisper secrets softly lush,
Palms sway gently, in a playful hush.
Squirrels giggle, acorns in hand,
While I try to dance but just can't stand!

Jungle Glow

Lizards lounge in sunbeam chairs,
Monkeys trade mischievous stares.
Mangoes drop while we do the cha,
And a parrot squawks, "La la la la!"

Spiders spin webs in disco balls,
While elephants wear sequined shawls.
Bees buzz jazz, in a blushing hue,
As butterflies join for a wacky crew!

Morning's Embrace

Roosters crow in synchronized beats,
As frogs croak out their tropical feats.
Giggling flowers sway to the tune,
And bees tap dance, under the moon.

With each ray a giggle, a flutter, a cheer,
The day awakens, oh so near.
Lemons wear sunglasses, just because,
In this silly, sunlit, paradise buzz!

Ethereal Horizons

The sun wore shades, oh what a sight,
A chubby cloud drifting with delight.
Fish in the sea are practicing breakdance,
While crabs hold auditions for their big chance.

Over there, the palm trees sway,
Singing to the breeze, come out to play!
A monkey slips, lands in the sand,
Winking at the waves, oh isn't life grand?

Seashells gossip, with tales so loud,
About the seagull who danced with the crowd.
Beach balls roll like tumbleweeds,
In this silly world of sunny misdeeds.

Bikinis laugh as they dry in the sun,
While flip-flops race, oh what a run!
A kite gets tangled in a coconut tree,
Making friends with a bee, all joy and glee.

Nature's Dance of Light

Butterflies wearing polka-dot coats,
Join the squirrels, who have great floats.
The sun's a jester, flickering bright,
Whispering secrets with all its might.

Chirping crickets in a conga line,
Sway to the rhythm, feeling divine.
A squirrel in shades, what a chic sight,
Grooving through branches, pure daylight.

Dancing shadows on a patch of green,
Wobbling around as if they're a scene.
A frog wearing socks sings a small tune,
Celebrating life beneath the full moon.

Raindrops giggle, they can't hold back,
Sliding on leaves, no sign of a track.
As the world twirls in laughter and jest,
Nature's a party, come be our guest.

Lightplay on the Leaves

The leaves giggle as the sun peeks through,
Making shadows play a merry debut.
A caterpillar's got moves so slick,
Busting a groove, ain't that quite the trick?

Branches sway with a playful air,
As bunnies hop without a care.
Fluffy clouds are laughing high,
Making faces, oh my, oh my!

A parrot squawks, wearing a crown,
Showing off feathers, never a frown.
Fireflies blink in a quirky dance,
Inviting the stars to join their prance.

The breeze tickles the flowers bright,
Whispers of joy, a sheer delight.
Every creature has a role to play,
In this shimmering, fun-filled display.

Coastal Echoes

Sea slugs waddle in tiny shoes,
Under the sun, singing the blues.
A pelican's strut, quite the grand show,
Wobbling around with a heavy flow.

The tides are chuckling, trying to tease,
Dancing with shells, just aim to please.
A crab, in a top hat, calls for a toast,
While the fish do flips, they're the ones to boast!

Sandcastles adorned with disco balls,
When the tide comes in, they have a ball.
A treasure map drawn on a napkin bright,
Leads to the candy store, oh what a sight!

Gulls in the air, cracking up jokes,
Delighting the kids, oh those little folks.
As day turns to evening, the fun sails away,
But memories linger, just come what may.

Gleam of Paradise

In a land where the sun likes to tease,
Coconuts chuckle in the warm, soft breeze.
Parrots gossip in colors so bright,
Dancing shadows play, full of delight.

Flip-flops squeak with each happy hop,
While the pineapples sit, never to stop.
A crab in a hat, oh, what a sight!
Sipping coconut juice, oh, it's pure delight!

Palm trees sway, like they're in on the joke,
Sunburned tourists laughing, they've gone up in smoke.
With drinks in their hands and sand on their skin,
Who knew paradise could be such a win!

The beach ball bounces while kiddos chase,
Belly flop contests bring smiles to each face.
As the sun sets low with a wink and a grin,
This gleam of joy invites everyone in.

Radiant Horizons

At dawn the roosters say, 'Rise and shine!'
While surfboards await their chance to align.
Flip over, flop down, splash in the sea,
The horizon chuckles, 'Come dance with me!'

Sandy toes wiggle, they start to groove,
Seashells compete in a game to improve.
A dolphin dives in, he's quite the clown,
With silly flips, he won't let you frown!

Sunscreen on noses, a white pasty treat,
Parents argue 'bout who gets the best seat.
But laughter drowns out the complaints in the air,
As everyone starts to dance without care!

Sunsets drip colors, pink, orange, and blue,
Each wave brings laughter, and a splash or two.
With radiant whispers, the evening ignites,
This charm of the coast serves pure comic delights!

Paradise in Bloom

Balloons float high, each petal's a smile,
A butterfly flutters, oh, what a style!
The flowers gossip, 'Did you see last night?'
As the bees chuckle, buzzing with delight.

The fruits in the market are dressed in their best,
Mangoes are laughing, they're just so blessed.
Watermelon slices giggle in a bowl,
As juicy laughter gives life to the soul.

Children play tag through gardens of cheer,
While sunlight pretends, 'I'm hiding right here!'
The carnival laughter is plentiful and loud,
As nature itself throws a jubilant crowd!

In this blooming comedy, all is alive,
Friendship and fun, oh how we thrive!
With each little moment, our spirits zoom,
In this vibrant corner, a paradise in bloom.

Swaying Shadows

Dancing on the sand, the shadows are sly,
As they twist and turn beneath the bright sky.
A lizard winks, and the coconuts smile,
Each creak and wiggle, it's all in style!

Old palm trees gossip about the breeze's tease,
Whispers of secrets float among the leaves.
Swaying left, swaying right, what a parade,
While the sun shakes its hips in a grand charade!

Kids in the waves, they splash and they shout,
The very ocean knows what laughter's about.
Crabs in a dance-off, pinching with flair,
Even the minnows join in with their care!

As twilight approaches, the shadows grow long,
With each silly dance, the joy feels so strong.
In this dappled comedy, the world twirls and spins,
Swaying shadows remind us where fun begins.

Waves of Gold

In the ocean's dance, waves prance,
A seagull's scream, a goofy chance.
Sunblock on my nose, white and bright,
Laughing as I slip, what a sight!

Beach chairs lined like soldiers at ease,
I wave at a crab; he waves back, please!
Sandcastles towering, all my pride,
Until a wave comes crashing, what a ride!

Ice cream melting quicker than tales,
Sticky fingers and beachy fails.
Sun hats flying with laughter's tune,
Dance like nobody, under the moon!

Flip-flops squeaking, what a sound,
I trip on a flip, and fall to the ground.
Yet there's joy in every sandy flip,
Life's a beach, let's all take a trip!

Sunkissed Breezes

Windy whispers, playful and light,
Sandy toes wiggle, what a sight!
Mangoes dripping, sticky sweet,
Fruit flies buzzing, can't take a seat!

A parrot squawks and steals my drink,
I chase him down, "Hey, stop to think!"
With every sip, laughter ignites,
Sunkissed antics, pure delights!

Palm trees sway to a calypso beat,
Barefoot dancing, joy's quick feet.
A kite gets tangled in my sun hat,
But I don't mind, just look at that!

Sunkissed wonders all around,
We laugh at how life spins round.
Embrace the giggles, let's be carefree,
In this sunny paradise, just you and me!

Radiant Reflections

Mirrors in the water, shimmering bright,
Fish making faces, quite a sight!
Splashing about, such brilliant fun,
A dive that ends with a face full of sun!

Clouds drift lazily, cotton-candy fluff,
Where is my towel? This is tough!
Sunscreen battles, slippery foes,
But oh, the laughter, it overflows!

Shadows of laughter dance on the shore,
Every silly moment, we adore.
Sun hats askew, smiles wide as can be,
Radiant joy glistens wild and free!

Bubbles float up as we blow and play,
Carefree moments slip softly away.
Yet memories linger with every wave,
Reflecting the joy that we all crave!

Lush Hues

In the jungle vibing, colors collide,
Bright butterflies flit, a joyous ride!
Lemons and limes, what a flavor burst,
Too much tang? Now I'm ready to burst!

An island beat, can you hear that sound?
Coconuts rolling, all around.
Grass skirts spinning, twirls so grand,
A dancing banana, who would've planned?

Palm fronds fluttering, a wacky parade,
Oh look, my hat's gone—the sun can invade!
Sipping on drinks with umbrellas that sway,
Every sip becomes a fun cliché!

The sunset paints laughter in warm hues,
Every giggle sparkles, it's all good news.
In this vibrant world where silly rules,
We dance like fools in our beachy jewels!

Emerald Echoes

In the jungle with a dance,
Lizards prance in their bright pants.
Parrots squawk with flair so grand,
Swinging from a leafy band.

Coconuts will drop from trees,
Landing gently with the breeze.
Monkeys giggle, causing fuss,
As if the world's a giant bus.

Frogs in tuxedos hop with glee,
Sipping nectar from a bee.
Nature's party, oh what fun!
Till the sun begins to run.

With emerald glimmers all around,
In this forest, joy is found.
Time to laugh and share a grin,
In the cheer where dreams begin.

Radiance in the Rainforest

Beneath the leaves, the shadows dance,
With cheeky monkeys making plans.
Sloths take naps, they've got the knack,
While toucans joke, "Who's got the snack?"

Rain drips down like a cool shower,
Plants all giggle, gaining power.
A blue butterfly flits with flair,
While ants march on like they don't care.

Lizards bask on hot rocks, too,
Sipping dew like it's brand new.
Frogs croon songs—a wild delight,
As croissants toast in morning light.

With colors bright and spirits high,
In this realm, the laughter flies.
Every corner, full of cheer,
What a place to spend your year!

Lush Luminescence

Sunbeams trickle through the trees,
Splashing smiles with every breeze.
A chameleon hides, turns to stone,
While iguanas claim the throne.

A samba rhythm fills the air,
As toucans strut without a care.
The caterpillars take a bow,
Saying, "We'll be butterflies now!"

The vibrant flowers wink and sway,
In this garden, come what may.
Bumblebees on a nectar chase,
Buzzing jokes—oh, what a race!

Even shadows join the fun,
Making shapes beneath the sun.
In lush lands, where giggles bloom,
Nature's laughter fills the room.

Serene Sunbeams

Golden rays are pure delight,
Chasing shadows, oh what sight!
Lizards lounge, a lazy crew,
Wondering what they'll get into.

Cacti wear their sunshine hats,
While goats dance like acrobats.
Pineapples grin, they're in the mix,
As palm trees tell their silly tricks.

The sun peeks through, the colors pop,
Making even the raindrops hop.
Frogs wear crowns made from the dew,
Hosting parties—everyone's due!

Every creature feels delight,
In this world where fun ignites.
So come and join this cheerful scene,
Laugh with us—it's fit for a queen!

www.ingramcontent.com/pod-product-compliance
Lightning Source LLC
Chambersburg PA
CBHW072216070526
44585CB00015B/1364